AF584368

A special thank you to everyone that helped make this book what it is:

My amazing husband Chris, my son Billy and his girlfriend Grace Smith for helping me.

Thank you also to the specialists who work in the field of grief and death who helped with the notes at the back of the book:

Nina King – art therapist working with children within families at hospices
Tilly Stevens – 'It All Matters', End of Life Planning, Education and Support
Elisabeth Price – for sharing the research for her thesis, Knowledge and perspectives on classroom conversations about death: A proactive and a reactive approach.

First published by Wildling Books in 2026.

Afterword notes by Rebekah Lipp. Book design by Wildling Books. Art design by Cheryl Smith.

A catalogue record for this book is available from the National Library of New Zealand.

ISBN 978-0-473-77078-5 (paperback)

Published by Wildling Books in 2026.
Printed in China by 1010 Printing International Limited.

Written by **Rebekah Lipp**
Illustrated by **Craig Phillips**

In the beginning, before you were you,
You shone so bright, with a light so true.

Bursting with love,
so warm, so bright ...

Connected to everything,
the day, the night.

Every living thing, big and small,
comes from the light that unites us all.

In a place beyond the
earth we know ...

Our unique wisp begins to glow.

The little glow falls gently down,
A perfect home that it has found.

Excited with a place to shine,

A ball of love from the divine.

Look around and a wisp you'll see,
shining brightly from within a tree.

In a loving hug, or your dog's cute face.
In every thing and every place.

Always there, that loving ray ...

Even on our darkest days.

As we walk along our path, we see,
Our journey creates memories.

We weave the light in all we do,
Learning, growing, and loving too.

The light within, so wise and true.

If we listen, it guides us too.

To walk with love, to live with grace.

To bring some love to every place.

A love so hard to comprehend,
we've forgotten how it all will end.
Return it must, the little glow.
Back home the clever light must go.

When someone dies, it is their turn.

No longer here, never to return.

Where did they go? Where could they be?
Your broken heart feels so heavy.

As their light dims, perhaps it sends
Tiny sparks to family and friends.

Pieces of love that decide to stay,
Joining our glow, finding their way.

One day this will happen to us all.
Our glow will leave, it's natural.

Is it the end? Or a new start?
Leaving will be the hardest part.

But when the time to part is near,
do not be sad, do not fear.

The light doesn't just fade away,
Cherished memories will always stay.

Look above and you will see,
lights that twinkle endlessly.

The love of those now far away,
still shining bright to light our way.

And deep inside, it's not just you,
those you've loved are all there too.
Their light lives on as part of you,
a gentle glow to guide you through.

PARENT/TEACHER NOTES

by Rebekah Lipp

Death will touch us all in one way or another. Sometimes death is expected, for example, when someone has had a long illness. Or if a beloved animal reaches an age where they won't live much longer. However, sometimes death can happen very unexpectedly. Talking about death is important as every living thing will die. As sad as that may seem, death is part of life, and some would say it is why life is so precious.

The Glow is a story I have held within me since I was a little girl. I always felt that I came from somewhere else and that I would return 'home' one day when I died. No one told me this, it is just something that I've felt in my heart from as early as I can remember. This is how I have processed the deaths of many people who I have loved. I look up at the stars and see my loved ones shine on me and then I feel them in my soul, my glow, my spirit. I know that one day I will join them when my time is right. This has helped ease the pain of losing those I have loved so much. I hope this book can help children do the same. I decided I needed to share this story when my eldest son, who was just five years old, realised that one day I too would die. It was a bittersweet moment to see his pure love for me as he cried and held onto me, while at the same time seeing the heartache and loss he would one day experience.

WHAT IS GRIEF?

Grief is a reaction or response to change and loss, for example when someone or something that we have formed a bond with, have affection for or is important to us dies. You can also grieve other things but in this book, we focus on grief in relation to the death of someone or something.

When someone or something we love dies, it can affect not just how we feel emotionally but also how we feel physically. Some people might find it hard to sleep or eat. Some people might cry a lot while others might not cry at all.

DID YOU KNOW THAT GRIEF IS NOT AN EMOTION?

Grief is our reaction to change and loss, which manifests in various emotions and behaviors, often several of them at the same time. Grief can manifest itself in many ways, like anger, sadness, anxiety, vivid memories, sleep disruption, shame, guilt, conflict with others, physical symptoms. Children will often display grief through their behaviours. They can sometimes act out of character when they are processing grief. It is important to meet them with compassion, just the same way as you would if they were crying.

It is also okay to feel positive emotions and/or laugh when grieving. Again, we all process grief differently and it doesn't make our grief any less hard. In my family we often laugh hysterically as a way to cope, which others sometimes find unusual, but it is just our way.

Different religions and cultures respond with death in different ways, and we hope this book can be moulded to the beliefs that you hold in your family.

For example, at the start of the book where it says, 'before you were you, you shone so bright with a light so true', you could talk about the light being God or a divine being – whatever works for your family.

Have you ever thought about death?

Has someone or something that you loved died?

What emotions did you feel?

Did the emotions change over days and weeks?

Everybody navigates grief and loss differently. There is no 'right way'. Emotions like anger can come up and that is normal.

Let children know that when someone dies, that person will not return. We might feel like we have a piece of them within us, their memories and their love, but the person that has died will never be able to return.

Because we all navigate death differently, we can sometimes clash over how we process our grief. If someone wants to talk about the person who died but another person doesn't want to, it can be difficult. Try to tell others how you want to process your grief. For example, try saying 'I want to talk about the person's death, who can I talk to?' Then ask those around you how they want to process this death. Remember that this can change over time. Always keep communicating about how you are processing your grief.

Children do find it hard to see adults close to them cry and be upset – that is not to say that adults should shield these emotions from them. Also, for example, if a child's mother or father dies, the child can then understandably become worried that the remaining parent will die and careful reassurances need to be made to the child.

WAYS TO REMEMBER THEM

We all like to remember people in different ways. Think about ways that are special for you. You could have a favourite photo in your room of them, or you could light a candle in a special spot to remember them. You could write to them or say a prayer for them. You could have a special toy or pillow that you hug when you are wanting a hug with the person/animal that has died.

Remember, they will always be with you, as part of your glow within, and in your precious memories. You can continue to love a person or animal who has died. You can relive the memories you have with them. You can talk about them, write in a journal about them, draw pictures and remember them in ways that work for you.

BE OPEN & HONEST WITH CHILDREN

It's okay for children to be curious about death. They may have questions about what happens when a person dies. Let them know they can ask any question about death, and you will do your best to answer them. Be as honest as possible, without gruelling details of course.

They need to ask questions so they can make sense of what has happened. They may ask the same question several times before they fully process the answer. Don't be afraid to use the words death, dying or dead. Avoid using words like passed away, lost, sleeping forever, gone away as this can be confusing for the child and make them think that the person might come back. There may be lots of new words that need explaining as well, for example, cemetery, cremation and ashes.

Let them know what is happening, so they understand changes in routines and where you are at, so they understand why you might be acting differently. It is okay to say "Sorry, I am really sad right now. Give me a minute and I'll be okay again; it is not your fault." Good role modelling of emotional skills is key! It is also okay to cry in front of them. Acknowledge that it is hard and sad, and that it's okay to feel angry or empty.

Be sure to let the people around your child know what has happened and ask them to be considerate of it.

Talking to children about death can be really uncomfortable for us adults as death might not have been discussed openly with us. Maybe we deal with death by not talking about it, so it can be difficult for us when our children want to talk about it.

Grief doesn't go away

A loved person's death will always be with us and the loss won't disappear. We will learn to cope with it better though. People often say "Our grief doesn't get smaller, but we grow around our grief."

We can also experience secondary losses, for example, going places that we used to go with that person, seeing things they loved, or hearing certain songs. Also, future events such as Christmas, birthdays, weddings and holidays can all bring grief back. This is totally normal.

Talking about death and grief helps

Externalising our emotions and thoughts through communication can help reduce their weight. It normalises them and brings them into our lives.

Grief changes us and our needs

We act, react, communicate and feel differently when grieving. It is a bit like being in a state of emergency. We have less tolerance and are more sensitive, which can easily lead to more fights, unfiltered communication and conflicts. Parents get snappy, kids get stroppy. If we are aware of this, we are more able to give ourselves and others some grace, kindness and patience.

WAYS TO SUPPORT GRIEVING CHILDREN

Give space

Children are often not that keen on talking. They need time and space to process, often hiding in their rooms doing their favorite activities and getting away from the adult chatter. That doesn't mean they're ignoring what has happened. In fact, they're actually practising self-care. Lots of children enjoy hanging out with their friends after someone has died because it gives them a sense of normality, not having to think or talk about it. Distraction can help us cope and is not a bad thing. It would all be too overwhelming otherwise.

Children also need to literally "move it" too: to go for a walk, take part in their teams' training, dance, jump or run. This helps them to reduce the tension in the body and release some of that energy.

Give hugs & be present

When it is hard to find the right words, physical warmth is great. Hang out together, sit on the couch next to one another, cuddle, snuggle and hug. Touch is a way of connection beyond words. Nurturing is essential in this most basic way. Let them know they can come to you when they need you, to talk or just hug or go for a walk. Or simply ask them to 'Tell you what you need.'

Make sure they know it is not their fault

Depending on their age kids tend to "fill in the gaps" in their mind if something doesn't add up. They might feel responsible for someone's death, if they can't explain it. They might feel responsible for your grief. They might feel that by crying they will make you even sadder. Let them know that they did not do this. It just happened and it is really hard but it is actually normal.

Don't minimize their grief

Sometimes parents and supporting adults can make a judgement about whether a child's grief is proportionate with their loss. For example, they might think that the child shouldn't be so upset about the loss they've experienced.

"Nothing that grieves us can be called little: by the eternal laws of proportion, a child's loss of a doll and a king's loss of a crown are events of the same size." Mark Twain.

Reach out

Use your community to support you! Grief is hard and better shared. If you become overwhelmed, it is okay to hand over your young person to a loving relative or friend, so you can organise yourself. You might want to look into grief support, too. Let your people know what you need and how they can help. Most people are more than happy to take the kids to the park, walk the dog, do a quick vacuum or bring a dinner! People tend to distance themselves if someone close to them is grieving. This is purely out of insecurity and not knowing what to say. It doesn't mean they don't care, but they feel unsure about how to help.what to say. It doesn't mean they don't care, but they feel unsure about how to help.

We have two other books that will work really well with this one. How Do I Feel? A dictionary of emotions with over 60 emotions, how they can feel in the body and how they might be helpful. This will be a good way to find the different emotions that come up during the grieving process.

The other is Let It Flow – healthy ways to release emotions. This book is filled with different ways to release the emotions that visit up in ways that won't hurt us or those around us.

The best books to compliment The Glow are:

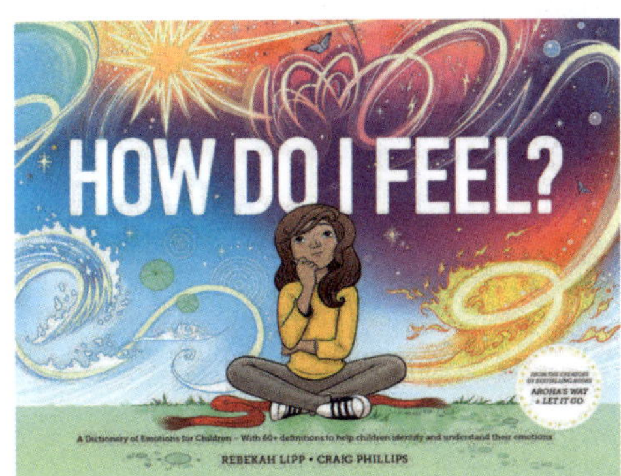

Check out the entire range at:

www.wildlingbooks.com